The BILL of RIGHTS

BY LUCIA RAATMA

CHILDREN'S PRESS®
An Imprint of Scholastic Inc.
New York Toronto London Auckland Sydney
Mexico City New Delhi Hong Kong
Danbury, Connecticut

BRINGING HISTORY to LIFE

Content Consultant
Rogers Smith, PhD
Christopher H. Brown
Distinguished Professor of Political Science
University of Pennsylvania
Philadelphia, Pennsylvania

Library of Congress Cataloging-in-Publication Data

Raatma, Lucia.
  The Bill of Rights/by Lucia Raatma.
    p. cm.—(Cornerstones of freedom)
  Includes bibliographical references and index.
  ISBN-13: 978-0-531-25027-3 (lib. bdg.) ISBN-10: 0-531-25027-X (lib. bdg.)
  ISBN-13: 978-0-531-26552-9 (pbk.)   ISBN-10: 0-531-26552-8 (pbk.)
  1. United States. Constitution. 1st–10th Amendments. 2. Civil Rights—
United States—History. I. Title.
  KF4750.R33 2012
  342.7308'5—dc22   2011009490

All rights reserved. Published in 2012 by Children's Press, an imprint of
Scholastic Inc.
Printed in China 62
SCHOLASTIC, CHILDREN'S PRESS, CORNERSTONES OF FREEDOM™,
and associated logos are trademarks and/or registered trademarks of
Scholastic Inc.

2 3 4 5 6 7 8 9 10 R 21 20 19 18 17 16 15 14 13

Photographs © 2012: Alamy Images: 20 (Tomas Abad), 37 (David R.
Frazier Photolibrary, Inc.), 2, 3, 47 (Kevin Shields), 36 (Stock Connection
Blue), 16 (Michael Ventura); AP Images: 19 (Diane Bondareff), 18 (Alan
Diaz), 29 (Ron Edmonds), 32 (Janet Hamlin), back cover (Andy Manis), 40
(Eric Risberg), 30 (Jim Urquhart), 38 (Dana Verkouteren), 4 top, 21, 51, 54;
Corbis Images/Bettmann: 50; Getty Images: 42 (Remy Gabalda/AFP), 41
(Frazer Harrison), 23 (Chris Hondros), 44 (Saul Loeb/AFP); iStockphoto/
Eliza Snow: cover; Library of Congress: 15, 57 (Constantino Brumidi), 13,
56 (Gilbert Stuart), 34; Lucia Raatma: 64; Media Bakery: 48 (Till Jacket), 35
(Tim Pannell), 33; National Archives and Records Administration: 5 bottom,
46; North Wind Picture Archives: 4 bottom, 5 top, 10, 12, 14, 22, 26, 27, 49,
58 top; Superstock, Inc./Junius Brutus Stearns: 11, 58 bottom, 59 bottom;
The Granger Collection, New York: 7, 59 top (Charles Willson Peale), 28
(ullstein bild), 8; The Image Works/Zach Ornitz/The Star-Ledger: 24.

Did you know that studying history can be fun?

BRING HISTORY TO LIFE by becoming a history investigator. Examine the evidence (primary and secondary source materials); cross-examine the people and witnesses. Take a look at what was happening at the time—but be careful! What happened years ago might suddenly become incredibly interesting and change the way you think!

Contents

Meeting the Needs of a New Government

In the 1600s, people from England began settling in North America. The colonists had few rights within the English government. They paid taxes but had no political voice. The colonists' frustration finally took the form of the American Revolutionary War (1775–1783).

The colonies became states and created a national legislature called the Confederation Congress. Soon, many thought they needed a stronger national government. Led by James Madison, the **Founding Fathers** gathered in 1787 to write the **U.S. Constitution**.

The Constitution was sent to the states to be **ratified** in September 1787. But many states were not sure that the Constitution fully guaranteed individual rights or states' rights. A respected politician from Virginia named George Mason had written the Declaration of Rights for his state's constitution. Many people believed that the U.S. Constitution needed something similar.

Nine states had ratified the Constitution by June 21, 1788. Four states still held out. A few days later, Virginia ratified the Constitution because of a promise from Madison that a bill of rights would be created. New York soon ratified the Constitution as well. North Carolina and Rhode Island refused.

The promise of a bill of rights helped win ratification. The final version of this document would come to be known as the Bill of Rights.

American colonists defeated the British in the American Revolutionary War. George Washington led the colonial army.

AS BILL OF RIGHTS DAY.

CHAPTER I

CREATING THE BILL OF RIGHTS

The first meeting of the Continental Congress took place in September 1774 in Philadelphia, Pennsylvania.

ONE OF THE BIGGEST

concerns the 13 states had as they reviewed and debated the U.S. Constitution was about the government's control. State leaders wanted to be sure that the national government's power would be limited. They also wanted to make sure citizens would still have basic personal freedoms.

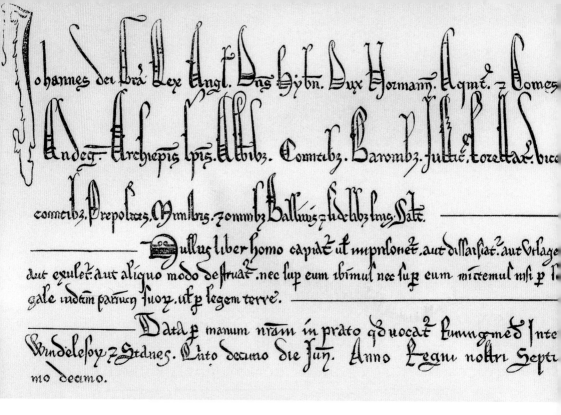

The Magna Carta listed the personal freedoms guaranteed to Englishmen.

The Magna Carta

Many historians believe that the Magna Carta served as an important basis for the Bill of Rights. Magna Carta means "Great Charter." It is a list of freedoms that was adopted in England in 1215.

This document states that the king of England is not above the law. He must follow the government's rules, just as everyone else is required to do.

King John approved the Magna Carta only after his noblemen and church leaders insisted that he do so. The Magna Carta assured the barons of their freedoms. It also guaranteed citizens the right to a fair legal system.

A FIRSTHAND LOOK AT
THE MAGNA CARTA

King Edward I approved an updated version of the Magna Carta in 1297. A copy is currently on display in the Rotunda Gallery at the National Archives and Records Administration in Washington, D.C. See page 60 for a link to view the document.

Many Ideas to Consider

The first Congress under the new U.S. Constitution met in New York City in April 1789. James Madison knew he had his work cut out for him. Many of the states had included separate bills of rights in their own constitutions. Each leader had many ideas to offer. More than 200 possible **amendments** had been submitted for consideration.

The Constitutional Convention met in Philadelphia in 1787 to create the U.S. Constitution.

Many people were eager for a bill of rights to be created. But Madison met some resistance. The Congress had so many issues to consider that some members did not feel that this bill should be a priority. Other members did not want anyone revising the Constitution at all.

Madison tried to introduce the bill of rights debate to the U.S. House of Representatives in May but was blocked. He made another attempt on June 8. He

George Washington was one of the leading speakers at the Constitutional Convention.

delivered an effective speech that got the legislators' attention. He convinced them that they owed the American people the time necessary to review the possible amendments. He also reminded them that two states had not yet ratified the Constitution and that unifying the states was an important matter. He then outlined what he thought the amendments should be.

Debating the Amendments

The House of Representatives sent the proposed amendments to a special committee six weeks after Madison's speech. The committee included one member from each state. The committee debated and made minor changes to Madison's list. They then sent it to the House. The

James Madison

James Madison has often been called the Father of the Constitution. But he maintained that many people contributed to the writing of this important document.

Madison was born in Orange County, Virginia. He studied law, history, and government at the College of New Jersey, which is now Princeton University. He helped create the Virginia Constitution. He also served in the Virginia Assembly. He took part in the Constitutional Convention in Philadelphia in 1787 and played a key role in getting the U.S. Constitution ratified.

Madison served as secretary of state while Thomas Jefferson was president. Madison was elected the fourth president of the United States in 1808.

Leaders of the new nation carefully discussed the creation of the Constitution.

members of the House approved the amendments on August 24.

That list was then sent to the U.S. Senate. The Senate debated the amendments even further. They decided to get rid of some of the amendments and combine others. This resulted in the approval of 12 amendments. The amendments were then sent to the individual states for review. Three-quarters of the states had to agree for the Bill of Rights to be approved. Two amendments were dropped. This made the final total 10. Those two amendments had more to do with Congress than with individual, local, or states' rights.

Maryland became the first state to ratify the Bill of Rights. Virginia was the ninth state to ratify it, on December 15, 1791. This fulfilled the three-quarters requirement. The Bill of Rights was born.

YESTERDAY'S HEADLINES

Alexander Hamilton objected to the idea of a Bill of Rights. In an article he wrote in *The Federalist Papers*—a publication that interpreted the Constitution—he asked, "For why declare that things shall not be done [by Congress] which there is no power to do? Why, for instance, should it be said that the liberty of the press shall not be restrained, when no power is given [to Congress] by which restrictions may be imposed?" Hamilton's argument was that it was not necessary to list all individual rights that the government should not have power over anyway. He also argued that such a list was dangerous. It could not possibly include every individual right.

CHAPTER 2

AMENDMENTS I AND II

The Bill of Rights guarantees all Americans freedom of religion.

THE MAIN GOAL OF THE BILL of Rights was to guard individual and state freedoms from excessive national power. The U.S. government plays an important part in keeping the nation operating. But many people wanted to be sure that the national government would not take away their rights. The first two amendments address individual and group rights to speech, assembly, religion, and personal protection.

Muslim men worship in Florida on the first day of Islam's holy period of Ramadan.

Amendment I

Congress shall make no law respecting an establishment of religion, or prohibiting the free exercise thereof; or abridging the freedom of speech, or of the press; or the right of the people peaceably to assemble, and to petition the government for a redress of grievances.

The First Amendment provides critical protections for U.S. citizens. It guarantees their right to practice any religion they choose. This is important because many other countries' governments tell their people what religion to follow. Many of the colonists came to America so they could practice religion freely. This idea was important to the Founding Fathers.

The phrase "shall make no law respecting an establishment of religion" has been interpreted in many different ways. One view is called separatism. Separatists believe that the government cannot endorse or support any religious establishment. Another view is called accommodationism. It argues that the government may support a religion as long as it treats all religions equally.

Jewish worshippers pray and celebrate the Jewish New Year, Rosh Hashanah, in New York City.

TODAY'S PERSPECTIVE

"...state shall...deny to any person within its jurisdiction the equal protection of the laws." —U.S. Constitution

On September 11, 2001, terrorists crashed airplanes into New York City's World Trade Center towers. The buildings were destroyed. Thousands of people were killed. The terrorists responsible for this tragedy were Muslims with radical ideas.

In 2010, a Muslim group announced plans to build a community center a few blocks away from where the World Trade Center once stood. Many Americans protested. They believed that such a building would be a terrible reminder of September 11, especially since it was Muslim terrorists who carried out the attacks. Other people argued that the First Amendment guarantees everyone the right to practice any religion they choose.

There is a third view called preferentialism. It claims that the government cannot establish a Church of America but can openly endorse Christianity.

The First Amendment protects people's rights to voice their own opinions by writing and speaking. This means that newspapers can publish editorials about any subject. It means that neighborhood leaders can complain about local rules. It also means that citizens can criticize government and call for change.

The First Amendment also guarantees citizens the right to meet in groups and to peacefully march and protest.

When police beat and teargassed peaceful protesters on March 7, 1965, they ignored the first amendment.

A FIRSTHAND LOOK AT
A CIVIL RIGHTS MARCH

On March 7, 1965, **civil rights** leaders began a peaceful march from Selma, Alabama, to the state capital in Montgomery. Their purpose was to protest unfair voting practices. The First Amendment supported their rights to free speech and assembly. But their rights were ignored. Local and state police beat the protesters and threw tear gas at them. This substance temporarily blinded them. The media reported their important story. The media had the right to report it under freedom of the press in the same amendment. The photographs taken of that day were shown all over the world. This brought attention to the civil rights issues in the United States. See page 60 for a link to view several photos.

Many of the American colonists who fought the British in the Revolutionary War belonged to militias, or nonprofessional groups of soldiers.

Amendment II

A well regulated militia, being necessary to the security of a free state, the right of the people to keep and bear arms, shall not be infringed.

What exactly did the Founding Fathers really mean when they created the Second Amendment? Did they mean that all citizens are allowed to own firearms? Or did they mean that the nation should have a national guard and a prepared military to protect citizens from attack? This issue continues to be hotly debated even today.

Many people believe the Second Amendment means that U.S. citizens have the right to own firearms to protect themselves. Others argue that too many guns are available to too many people in the United States. Some leaders worry that giving everyone access to machine guns and other military-grade machinery is dangerous. But others insist that owning guns is a right protected by the Second Amendment.

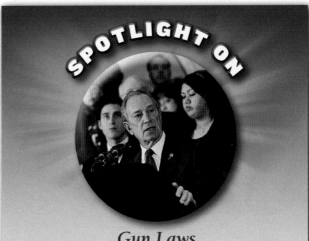

SPOTLIGHT ON

Gun Laws

Current gun regulations are intended to prevent people with criminal records and mental health issues from buying guns. But store owners who sell firearms do not always enforce these laws. Mayor Michael Bloomberg of New York City is the chair of Mayors Against Illegal Guns. He began a campaign in 2011 to strengthen gun control laws.

Mayor Bloomberg expressed his thoughts about guns in the United States on a national television program in February 2011, saying, "Every day, 34 Americans are murdered with guns, and most of them are purchased or possessed illegally. It is time for Washington to . . . take action."

CHAPTER 3

AMENDMENTS III AND IV

Citizens can be questioned by law enforcement officers, but the Bill of Rights protects Americans from "unreasonable searches and seizures" of their property.

THE THIRD AND FOURTH

Amendments focus on the rights of U.S. citizens in their homes. Many people today take the privacy of their homes for granted. But throughout history, people have often had to protect their residences and possessions. Today, people in some nations may have their belongings taken by the government. There is little that they can do to fight it. The Bill of Rights prevents that kind of injustice in the United States.

In the years before the Revolutionary War, British soldiers were often housed in colonists' homes.

Amendment III

No soldier shall, in time of peace be quartered in any house, without the consent of the owner, nor in time of war, but in a manner to be prescribed by law.

This amendment states that U.S. citizens do not have to allow soldiers to live in their homes. This may not seem like an important issue today. But a different situation existed in the colonies during the 1700s. Britain fought France for control of North America from 1756 to 1763. British soldiers often lived in the private homes of Americans during that time. The colonists were powerless to prevent quartering troops. The continuing practice became a large source of tension between the colonies and Britain.

SPOTLIGHT ON

The Quartering Acts

The first Quartering Act was passed by the British Parliament in 1765. It required that British troops be given food and lodging in the American colonies. The troops were to be allowed to stay at inns and barracks, which are official military quarters, and houses. The colonists had to pay for the cost of hosting the soldiers. Another Quartering Act was passed in 1774, as part of the Intolerable Acts. Britain enacted these laws to strengthen its control of the American colonies. But the laws only angered and frustrated the colonists further.

Amendment IV

The right of the people to be secure in their persons, houses, papers, and effects, against unreasonable searches and seizures, shall not be violated, and no warrants shall issue, but upon probable cause, supported by oath or affirmation, and particularly describing the place to be searched, and the persons or things to be seized.

YESTERDAY'S HEADLINES

In Germany during the 1930s, a knock at the door struck fear in the people living in the house. This was because German leader Adolf Hitler had a strong hatred of the Jewish people. He wanted to eliminate them. He ordered Nazi soldiers to search homes and round up Jews. The Jews were then sent to concentration camps. They were forced into labor or killed at these camps. Nazis also were known for arresting anyone who helped hide or assist Jews.

The Fourth Amendment protects U.S. citizens from random searches of their homes.

The Fourth Amendment protects citizens from having their homes or possessions taken by the government. It also prevents officials from searching private homes and businesses without a good reason.

Police officers can search homes and businesses under certain circumstances. Usually this is true when illegal materials are in plain sight or if a person grants the police permission to search. In many cases police officers must obtain a **warrant** before they can search someone's home or office. This means they have to explain to a judge what the threat is and get the judge's permission to search.

In 2001, President George W. Bush signed into law the USA Patriot Act to fight terrorism. Some opponents of the act believe it threatens the Fourth Amendment rights of Americans.

A FIRSTHAND LOOK AT
THE PAPERS OF JAMES MADISON

James Madison once explained, "In a word, as a man is said to have a right to his property, he may be equally said to have a property in his rights." These and other writings can be found in *The Papers of James Madison*, a project maintained by the University of Virginia. The University of Chicago published the first 10 volumes. The University of Virginia Press has produced the remaining volumes. See page 60 for a link to view several of Madison's original handwritten documents.

CHAPTER 4

AMENDMENTS V AND VI

The Bill of Rights guarantees a fair and timely trial by jury to even those accused of the most serious crimes.

THE FIFTH AND SIXTH AMENDMENTS

work to protect the rights of people accused of a crime. People in the United States are presumed innocent unless they are proven guilty of a crime. This means it is important to guarantee the rights of people while they are being investigated or tried by a jury.

Juries are rarely photographed during a trial. Instead, courtroom artists make sketches of the jury, lawyers, and judges to inform the public about a trial's proceedings.

Amendment V

No person shall be held to answer for a capital, or otherwise infamous crime, unless on a presentment or indictment of a grand jury, except in cases arising in the land or naval forces, or in the militia, when in actual service in time of war or public danger; nor shall any person be subject for the same offense to be twice put in jeopardy of life or limb; nor shall be compelled in any criminal case to be a witness against himself, nor be deprived of life, liberty, or property, without due process of law; nor shall private property be taken for public use, without just compensation.

A capital crime is one that can be punished by death. An infamous crime is one that results in a prison sentence and loss of rights. The Fifth Amendment protects people from having to be on trial for such a crime unless they have first been **indicted** by a grand jury. This means the grand jury agrees that there is a good reason to hold a trial.

This amendment also prevents a person from being tried for the same crime twice. If a man is proven not guilty of a murder, he cannot be tried again for that

Jurors listen carefully to testimony from witnesses who provide information about the case.

Elizabeth Cady Stanton was an important leader of the 19th-century women's rights movement in the United States.

murder, even if more evidence is presented. But a person can be tried again if a legal error was made. The Fifth Amendment guarantees a person a fair trial. This means a government cannot simply declare people guilty and sentence them to jail. The amendment also says that people do not have to provide information against themselves.

A FIRSTHAND LOOK AT

THE SELECTED PAPERS OF ELIZABETH CADY STANTON AND SUSAN B. ANTHONY

In 1873, a New York judge found Susan B. Anthony guilty for voting at a time when women did not yet have the right to vote. The judge asked if she had anything to say. "Yes, your honor," replied Miss Anthony. "I have many things to say. My every right, constitutional, civil, political and judicial has been tramped upon. I have not only had no jury of my peers, but I have had no jury at all." Her story is collected in *The Selected Papers of Elizabeth Cady Stanton and Susan B. Anthony*. See page 60 for a link to the text of her trial.

Attorneys sometimes speak directly to the jury.

Amendment VI

In all criminal prosecutions, the accused shall enjoy the right to a speedy and public trial, by an impartial jury of the state and district wherein the crime shall have been committed, which district shall have been previously ascertained by law, and to be informed of the nature and cause of the accusation; to be confronted with the witnesses against him; to have compulsory process for obtaining witnesses in his favor, and to have the assistance of counsel for his defense.

Each jury has a foreperson, or leader, who reads the jury's decisions in the courtroom.

The Sixth Amendment guarantees people the right to a fair trial. It also says a trial has to take place in a timely manner. This keeps accused people from waiting in jail for too long. The Sixth Amendment also provides that the location of a trial can be moved if a person cannot get a fair trial in a given area. This can happen if a story has been in the local news so much that potential jury members have already made up their minds about the crime.

The Founding Fathers knew that a "public trial" could greatly embarrass someone accused of a crime as details of the case were revealed. Yet they also knew that a public trial would be less likely to be conducted in an unfair manner.

Defendants, or people accused of a crime, are entitled to jury trials. Juvenile defendants are not. This is done to protect their privacy.

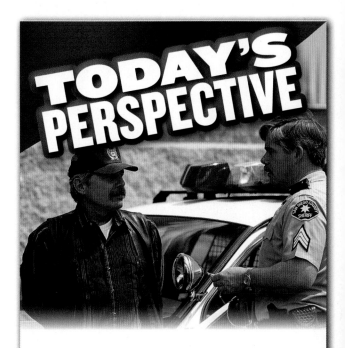

TODAY'S PERSPECTIVE

"You have the right to remain silent. Anything you say can and will be used against you in a court of law. You have the right to speak to an attorney. If you cannot afford an attorney, one will be appointed for you. Do you understand these rights as they have been read to you?"

Those words make up the Miranda rights. This important statement must be read to people when they are arrested. In the 1966 Supreme Court case *Miranda v. Arizona*, the judges declared that Ernesto Miranda had not received a fair trial because he did not know he could refuse to talk to authorities or that he had a right to an attorney. The Miranda rights were a result of this case.

CHAPTER 5

AMENDMENTS VII AND VIII

The Seventh and
Eighth Amendments
address trial by jury and
limitations on bail.

THE SEVENTH AND EIGHTH

Amendments also protect the rights of people who are accused or convicted of crimes. These amendments set standards for jury trials and set limits on **bail**. The Eighth Amendment also focuses on how an accused person should be treated when on trial.

Many people accused of crimes cannot afford bail, so they are jailed.

Amendment VII

In suits at common law, where the value in controversy shall exceed twenty dollars, the right of trial by jury shall be preserved, and no fact tried by a jury, shall be otherwise reexamined in any court of the United States, than according to the rules of the common law.

The Seventh Amendment protects the rights of people involved in a **civil suit**, which is about personal matters. The government is always the prosecutor in a **criminal case**. In a civil case, two people face each other. This amendment states that whatever decision a jury makes must be observed. The decision cannot be argued again later, even if other people disagree with it. An exception is if an **appeals court** decides that common law has not been followed. Common law refers to the rules established in past cases.

Small-Claims Court

How much was $20 in 1791? It would equal about $500 today. Most modern civil cases result in decisions worth more than $20. If a person has a civil case that involves rewards of as much as a few thousand dollars, he or she probably won't have a jury trial. That person is more likely to go to small-claims court instead. The laws vary from state to state. Most small-claims courts handle cases that award up to $5,000. In most cases, a judge hears from the defendant and then decides which party is right.

Amendment VIII

Excessive bail shall not be required, nor excessive fines imposed, nor cruel and unusual punishments inflicted.

Many people around the world hold protests to show their disagreement with the death penalty.

A person charged with a crime sometimes has to pay bail. This is a fee paid to the court. It is much like a deposit. Bail allows a person to stay out of jail while waiting for his or her trial to begin. The fee is returned if the person appears at the trial as promised. The fee is lost if the person flees the state or country to avoid the trial. The Eighth Amendment prevents courts from setting unreasonably large bail amounts. The amounts depend on the type of crime committed. A person accused of murder would receive a higher bail than someone accused of stealing a car.

The Eighth Amendment also protects people from excessive punishment, such as mental or physical torture. Inhumane prison conditions are also prohibited by the Eighth Amendment. Interpretation of "cruel and unusual punishments," which appears in the amendment, has changed over time. The Crimes Act of 1790 ordered the death penalty for treason but also stated that the bodies of executed convicted murderers could be mutilated. Floggings, or beatings with a whip, were also common at the time. Both practices would be considered cruel and unusual forms of punishment today.

A VIEW FROM ABROAD

The Eighth Amendment was intended to prevent cruel and unusual punishment. But what about the death penalty? Many people believe that being put to death for a crime is the cruelest punishment possible. Supporters of the death penalty say that the practice rids society of its worst criminals. Those opposed to the death penalty argue that life in prison is more humane. They also argue that some prisoners who were on death row have since been proven innocent and freed.

Many states in the United States still have the death penalty as a possible choice of punishment. But most countries in Europe have outlawed the practice.

CHAPTER 6

AMENDMENTS IX AND X

The Ninth and Tenth Amendments limit the power of the federal government.

THE LAST TWO AMENDMENTS in the Bill of Rights offer broad protections to U.S. citizens. They are intended to keep individual rights and allow states certain rights that do not fall under federal powers. The Ninth Amendment in particular addresses the fears that Alexander Hamilton expressed in *The Federalist Papers*.

The original Bill of Rights has been preserved in Washington, D.C.

Amendment IX

The enumeration in the Constitution, of certain rights, shall not be construed to deny or disparage others retained by the people.

This amendment admits that the Constitution does not list all of the rights Americans have. But this does not mean that people do not deserve those rights.

A FIRSTHAND LOOK AT
THE U.S. CONSTITUTION

The U.S. Constitution is the oldest written constitution that is still being used by a nation. Jacob Shallus, a clerk from the Pennsylvania General Assembly, is credited with handwriting the document. Along with the **Declaration of Independence** and the Bill of Rights, it is on permanent display in the Rotunda for the Charters of Freedom at the National Archives Building in Washington, D.C. See page 60 for a link to the original four-page document.

Many people travel to the National Archives in Washington, D.C., to see documents such as the Bill of Rights and the Constitution.

A Right to Privacy

Legal cases over the years have supported people's individual rights to privacy. Many people believe that the First Amendment (freedom of belief), Third Amendment (right to protect the home), and Fourth Amendment (right to prevent illegal search and seizure) all address different forms of privacy. The Ninth Amendment offers a wide interpretation of rights, which could include privacy. These privacy ideals have been supported in cases that protect information about a person's medical condition or a person's decision about medical treatment.

People are due individual and group rights, whether they are outlined in the Constitution or not.

The Ninth Amendment helps show how the Founding Fathers viewed the liberties they anticipated Americans would enjoy under the Constitution. The Founding Fathers knew they were not creating liberties in the Bill of Rights. They believed they were simply recognizing some of the rights that no government could deny.

Amendment X

The powers not delegated to the United States by the Constitution, nor prohibited by it to the states, are reserved to the states respectively, or to the people.

This amendment limits the power of the federal government. It states that any powers not granted to the U.S. government or prohibited to the states can be

James Madison correctly predicted that there would eventually be a conflict over states' rights.

controlled by individual states and the people. This means that certain laws can vary from state to state. But state laws should be in keeping with the U.S. Constitution.

When Madison was listing his proposed amendments in 1789, the Senate rejected what he called the "most valuable amendment." This amendment limited states'

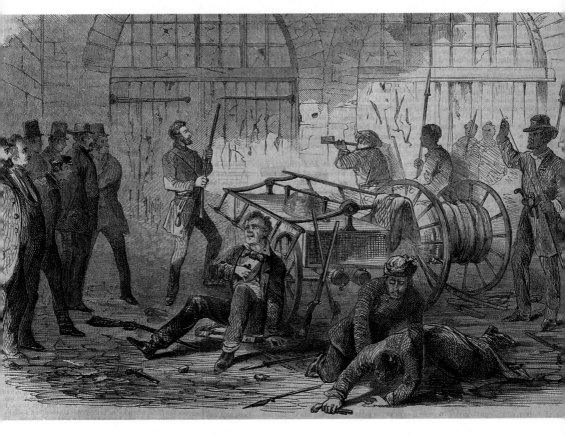

The argument over slavery often resulted in violence, even before the Civil War.

powers if they violated individual rights. This issue
came to a head regarding the practice of slavery. Some
states began to outlaw slavery. Other states decided to
keep it legal. Some leaders argued that states had the
constitutional right to do this. Others contended that
slavery violated individual rights and therefore was
unconstitutional. This debate continued during the Civil
War and was finally resolved with further amendments
to the Constitution.

YESTERDAY'S HEADLINES

Jim Crow Laws

There are many examples of state laws that have proven to be unconstitutional. One example is the Jim Crow laws. These laws were in effect in several states between 1876 and 1965. **Segregation** of white and black citizens was required under these laws. Black people had to sit in separate areas in train stations, movie theaters, and restaurants. Many were forced to attend schools separate from white students.

The Jim Crow laws were governed by individual states. But they violated the rights of black citizens. In 1954, many Jim Crow laws were overturned in the *Brown v. Board of Education of Topeka* case. This case declared that public schools could no longer be segregated.

What Happened Where?

Pennsylvania: December 12, 1787
March 10, 1790

Maryland: April 28, 1788
December 19, 1789

Virginia: June 25, 1788
December 15, 1791

North Carolina: November 21, 1789
December 22, 1789

South Carolina: May 23, 1788
January 19, 1790

Georgia: January 2, 1788
March 18, 1792

SC

GA

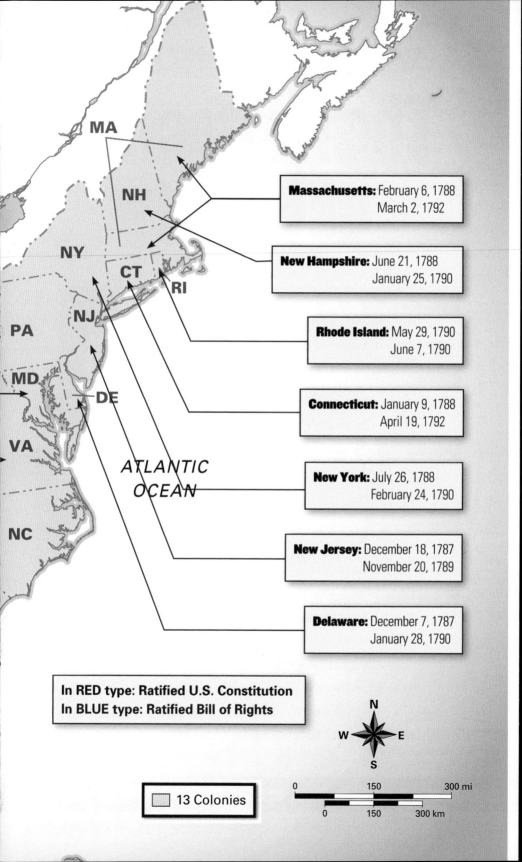

MA

NH

NY

CT

RI

NJ

PA

MD

DE

VA

NC

ATLANTIC
OCEAN

Massachusetts: February 6, 1788
March 2, 1792

New Hampshire: June 21, 1788
January 25, 1790

Rhode Island: May 29, 1790
June 7, 1790

Connecticut: January 9, 1788
April 19, 1792

New York: July 26, 1788
February 24, 1790

New Jersey: December 18, 1787
November 20, 1789

Delaware: December 7, 1787
January 28, 1790

In RED type: Ratified U.S. Constitution
In BLUE type: Ratified Bill of Rights

N
W   E
S

0   150   300 mi
0   150   300 km

☐ 13 Colonies

THE STORY CONTINUES

The Protection of Liberty

During World War II, many American citizens of Japanese descent were sent to relocation camps by the U.S. government.

The Constitution and Bill of Rights attempt to protect the rights of every citizen. But this goal is often hard to achieve. It has often taken many years to recognize the rights of all Americans.

TODAY, THERE ARE 27 AMENDMENTS

Slavery was not outlawed until 1865, when the 13th Amendment was passed. Three years later, the 14th Amendment guaranteed the rights of all citizens, regardless of race, belief, status, or wealth. The right to vote was extended beyond white people in 1870. But it took until 1920, with the 19th Amendment, for women to be granted the right to vote.

Upholding the Bill of Rights has sometimes proved challenging. One example occurred during World War II (1939–1945). Many Americans grew suspicious of Japanese American citizens after Pearl Harbor, Hawaii, was attacked by the Japanese military. Many Japanese Americans were sent to internment camps during the war without being charged with any crimes. They were put in these camps simply for having a Japanese background.

The U.S. government has sometimes been accused of exceeding its powers. The government passed the USA Patriot Act after the September 11 terrorist attacks. This law gave government and law enforcement officials increased power to search individuals' financial and medical records, as well as access telephone conversations and e-mails. A hot debate continues as to whether this law is constitutional or not.

It has been the responsibility of the U.S. government and its people since 1791 to preserve the Constitution, uphold the Bill of Rights, and protect the freedoms of all citizens. These responsibilities remain to this day.

INFLUENTIAL INDIVIDUALS

King John (1167–1216) was the son of King Henry II and Eleanor of Aquitaine. He became king of England in 1199 and approved the Magna Carta in 1215.

George Mason (1725–1792) was a statesman from Virginia, one of the Founding Fathers, and a delegate to the U.S. Constitutional Convention of 1787. He wrote the Declaration of Rights for his state, a document that influenced the Bill of Rights.

Thomas Jefferson (1743–1826) was the main author of the Declaration of Independence. He is considered one of the Founding Fathers and served as third president of the United States.

Jacob Shallus (1750–1796) was a clerk in the Pennsylvania General Assembly. He is responsible for handwriting the U.S. Constitution.

James Madison (1751–1836) was one of the Founding Fathers. He was the main author of the U.S. Constitution and led the effort for a U.S. Bill of Rights. He served as the fourth president of the United States.

James Madison

Alexander Hamilton (ca. 1755–1804) was a Founding Father and later served as U.S. secretary of the treasury. With James Madison, he wrote most of *The Federalist Papers*, which interpreted the U.S. Constitution.

Alexander Hamilton

Susan B. Anthony (1820–1906) worked to help women win the right to vote in the United States. In 1873, she was found guilty of voting illegally.

Ernesto Arturo Miranda (1941–1976) was arrested and questioned by police in 1963. He confessed to his crimes, but police did not inform him that he had the right to a lawyer and the right to remain silent. His case went before the Supreme Court and resulted in the adoption of the Miranda rights in 1966.

TIMELINE

1215
Magna Carta accepted in England

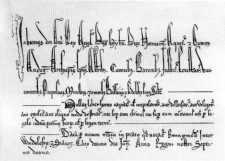

1765
First Quartering Act passed

1774
Second Quartering Act passed

1787
U.S. Constitution written

1775

American Revolutionary War begins

1776

George Mason drafts the Declaration of Rights for the Virginia Constitution

1783

Revolutionary War ends with the Siege of Yorktown

1789

First draft of the U.S. Bill of Rights written

1791

U.S. Bill of Rights ratified

LIVING HISTORY

Primary sources provide firsthand evidence about a topic. Witnesses to a historical event create primary sources. They include autobiographies, newspaper reports of the time, oral histories, photographs, and memoirs. A secondary source analyzes primary sources, and is one step or more removed from the event. Secondary sources include textbooks, encyclopedias, and commentaries.

The Civil Rights Movement in the United States In March 1965, three very important civil rights protests took place in Alabama. View photos of the marches and read about the protesters' eventual arrival in Montgomery at *www.cr.nps.gov/nr/travel/civilrights /cost.htm*

The Elizabeth Cady Stanton and Susan B. Anthony Papers Project Susan B. Anthony was a suffragette, a woman fighting to get voting rights for women in the United States. To read the text of a trial that found her guilty of voting without the right, go to *http:// ecssba.rutgers.edu/docs/sbatrial.html*

The Magna Carta A copy of the Magna Carta can be seen in person at the Rotunda Gallery at the National Archives and Records Administration in Washington, D.C. To view the document, go to *www.archives.gov/exhibits/featured_documents/magna_carta/*

The Papers of James Madison James Madison was the Father of the U.S. Constitution. To read his thoughts on the government of the new country, go to *http://press-pubs.uchicago.edu/founders /documents/v1ch16s23.html* and see *www.virginia.edu/pjm /mad-docs1.htm* for Madison's handwritten documents.

The U.S. Constitution The U.S. Constitution is on permanent display at the National Archives Building. To view the original four-page document, go to *www.archives.gov/exhibits/charters /constitution_zoom_1.html*

Books

Gaines, Ann. *James Madison: Our Fourth President*. Chanhassen, MN: The Child's World, 2009.

Landau, Elaine. *The Declaration of Independence*. New York: Children's Press, 2008.

Murphy, Jim. *The Crossing: How George Washington Saved the American Revolution*. New York: Scholastic Press, 2010.

Pederson, Charles E. *The U.S. Constitution & Bill of Rights*. Edina, MN: Abdo Publishing Company, 2010.

Stanton, Terence M. *The Bill of Rights: What It Means to You*. New York: Rosen Publishing Group, 2009.

Taylor-Butler, Christine. *The Bill of Rights*. New York: Children's Press, 2008.

Web Sites

Library of Congress: The Bill of Rights
www.loc.gov/rr/program/bib/ourdocs/billofrights.html
This site provides background to the Bill of Rights and links to a number of related primary documents.

Rotunda for the Charters of Freedom
www.archives.gov/nae/visit/rotunda.html
Visit the permanent home of the Declaration of Independence, the U.S. Constitution, and the Bill of Rights.

The United States Constitution
http://constitutionus.com/
This site provides the text of the Constitution and its amendments.

GLOSSARY

amendments (uh-MEND-muhnts) changes that are made to a law or a legal document

appeals court (uh-PEELZ KORT) a type of court that can reconsider a case and overturn its outcome if mistakes were made

bail (BALE) a sum of money paid to a court that prevents a person from having to stay in jail until his or her trial starts

civil rights (SIV-il RITES) the individual rights that all members of society have, including freedom and equal treatment under the law

civil suit (SIV-il SOOT) a court case that is personal and does not involve criminal activity

criminal case (KRIM-uh-nuhl KAYSS) a court case that involves the government charging someone with a crime

Declaration of Independence (dek-luh-RAY-shuhn UHV in-di-PEN-duhnss) a document that declared the freedom of the 13 colonies from British rule

Founding Fathers (FOUND-ihng FAH-thurz) the leading figures in the creation of the United States

indicted (in-DITE-id) officially charged with a crime

ratified (RAT-uh-fyed) agreed to or approved officially

segregation (seg-ruh-GAY-shuhn) the act of separating people based on race, gender, or other factors

U.S. Constitution (YOO ESS kahn-sti-TOO-shuhn) a document that contains the U.S. system of laws, including all the rights of the people and the responsibilities of the government

warrant (WOR-uhnt) an official document that gives permission for something, such as searching or arresting someone

Page numbers in *italics* indicate illustrations.

ABOUT THE AUTHOR

Lucia Raatma earned a bachelor's degree from the University of South Carolina and a master's degree from New York University. She has authored dozens of books for young readers and particularly enjoys writing about American history. She is inspired by the Bill of Rights and is most grateful for the First Amendment. For more information, visit *www.luciaraatma.com.*